FOR YOU, WITH A
SMILE

YURI ANJOS

Cover photo by Deisiane Rodrigues

To order additional copies of this book, contact:
Xlibris
1-888-795-4274
www.Xlibris.com
Orders@Xlibris.com

ISBN: Softcover   978-1-7960-6703-3
        EBook   978-1-7960-6702-6

Print information available on the last page

Rev. date: 11/18/2019

A
SMILE

That simple yet automatic movement
of my lips when I see you

Or an ear to ear beam like

when you first said yes

A smile is so beautiful and welcoming that we can't help but want to see them more and more.

It can be felt from far away,

But its splendor is incomparable to when we are close

So close that I can feel the

warmth of your breath

Why?

I see your letters

I see your sleepy morning face next to mine

So, wear yours more often.

Spread it to the World, and see how
you will change lives and move mountains
with a simple smile. Your smile.

Printed in the United States
By Bookmasters